The Firs

A Beginner's Guide to Making and Screening Your First Short Film

ISBN: 9798327136328
Independently Published.

Copyright © 2024 by Steve McCarten

All rights reserved. No part of this book may be reproduced, distributed, or transmitted in any form or by any means, including photocopying, recording, or other electronic or mechanical methods, without the prior written permission of the publisher, except in the case of brief quotations embodied in critical reviews and certain other non-commercial uses permitted by copyright law. For permission requests, write to the publisher via the web form found on www.stevemccarten.com

Disclaimer

The information contained in this book is for general informational purposes only. While the author has made every effort to ensure the accuracy and completeness of the information provided, they assume no responsibility for errors, inaccuracies, omissions, or any other inconsistencies herein. Any reliance you place on such information is strictly at your own risk.

The author shall not be liable for any loss or damage, including but not limited to indirect or consequential loss or damage, or any loss or damage whatsoever arising from the use of this book or the reliance on any information contained within it.

This book contains links to external websites that are not provided or maintained by or in any way affiliated with the author. Please note that the author does not guarantee the accuracy, relevance, timeliness, or completeness of any information on these external websites.

By using this book, you agree to indemnify, defend, and hold harmless the author from and against any and all claims, liabilities, damages, losses, or expenses (including attorneys' fees and costs) arising out of or in any way connected with your use of this book and the information contained herein.

For professional advice and specific guidance regarding your film projects, it is recommended to consult directly with industry professionals or other reliable sources.

Introduction

Welcome to "The First Frame: A Beginner's Guide to Making and Screening Your First Short Film." My name is Steve McCarten, and I am thrilled to guide you through the exciting journey of filmmaking. With several short films under my belt, including "Faithless," which has garnered awards at international film festivals, and extensive experience in various TV and film roles, I am here to share my knowledge and passion for storytelling with you.

Why This Book?

Filmmaking can seem like a daunting task, especially when you're just starting out. The process involves a myriad of steps, from developing an idea to editing the final cut. This book aims to demystify that process, breaking it down into manageable, step-by-step instructions that will help you navigate each stage with confidence.

You might be wondering why another book on filmmaking is necessary. The answer lies in the unique approach we take here. This book is not just about the technical aspects of filmmaking; it's about embracing the journey, learning from each step, and, most importantly, enjoying the creative process. We'll provide concrete techniques and tools, but we'll also share anecdotes and insights that will keep you motivated and inspired.

Overview of the Book

The structure of this book mirrors the filmmaking process itself, divided into clear, actionable chapters:

- The Spark of an Idea: Discover how to find inspiration and develop a compelling story.

- Scriptwriting for Short Films: Learn the basics of screenwriting, from structure to character development.

- Pre-Production Planning: Understand the importance of planning, budgeting, and assembling your team.

- Storyboarding and Shot Planning: Visualize your film through storyboards and shot lists.

- Location Scouting and Set Preparation: Find and prepare the perfect locations for your shoot.

- Equipment and Technical Basics: Get to grips with the essential equipment and technical know-how.

- Directing Your Short Film: Learn how to communicate your vision and work with actors.

- Filming Your Short Film: Master on-set protocols and efficient shooting techniques.

- Editing Your Short Film: Dive into the editing process to create a polished final product.

- Post-Production Essentials: Finalize your film with colour correction, sound mixing, and visual effects.

- Preparing for the Screening: Plan and execute a successful premiere.

- Navigating Film Festivals and Distribution: Learn how to submit your film to festivals and distribute it effectively.

The Importance of Storytelling

At its core, filmmaking is about storytelling. It's about sharing a piece of your vision with the world and connecting with your audience on an emotional level. Whether your story is a heartfelt drama, a thrilling mystery, or a whimsical comedy, this book will help you bring your unique voice to life. We'll guide you through the process of crafting a narrative that resonates and leaves a lasting impact.

My Personal Journey

Allow me to share a bit about my own journey into filmmaking. Like many of you, I started with a simple idea and a lot of passion. My first short film was far from perfect, but it was a labour of love that taught me invaluable lessons. I faced countless challenges – from budget constraints to technical difficulties – but each obstacle was an opportunity to learn and grow. Over the years, I have had the good fortune to work on various projects, including "Faithless," "FutureTX," and "Season 2 of Trigger Point," gaining experience in directing, producing, and writing. Additionally, I have taught BA Media Production, BATV, and MA Directing and MA Producing at Bournemouth University, further enriching my understanding of the craft.

What You Will Gain

By the end of this book, you will have:

A solid understanding of the entire filmmaking process.

The ability to create a compelling short film script.

Practical skills in pre-production planning, directing, and editing. Knowledge of how to attract collaborators and build a strong team. Strategies for marketing and screening your film. More importantly, you'll gain the confidence to take your first steps in the world of filmmaking and the inspiration to keep pushing forward, no matter the challenges.

How to Use This Book

This book is designed to be both a reference guide and a hands-on workbook. Each chapter includes exercises and practical tips that you can apply directly to your project. I encourage you to take your time with each section, experiment with the techniques, and adapt them to suit your unique style and vision.

As you embark on this journey, remember that filmmaking is as much about the process as it is about the final product.

Embrace the learning curve, celebrate your progress, and most importantly, enjoy the creative adventure.

Chapter 1: The Spark of an Idea

Finding Inspiration

Inspiration is the lifeblood of creativity, and for filmmakers, it often comes from the most unexpected places. Whether it's a captivating scene in a classic film or an intriguing conversation overheard in a café, ideas can spring from anywhere. For me, the works of Alfred Hitchcock and Steven Spielberg have been monumental. Hitchcock's meticulous blocking of actors and camera to convey the tension between characters, as seen in "Vertigo," and Spielberg's dynamic camera movements to enhance storytelling, serve as perpetual sources of inspiration.

Great filmmakers often draw inspiration from a variety of sources. Quentin Tarantino, for instance, is known for his vast knowledge of films and his ability to blend genres. In an interview, he once said, "I steal from every movie ever made." This highlights the importance of watching and learning from a wide range of films.

Exercise: Identifying Your Inspirations

List Your Inspirations:

Directors: Alfred Hitchcock, Steven Spielberg, Quentin Tarantino, Sofia Coppola, Martin Scorsese.

Films: "Vertigo," "Jaws," "Pulp Fiction," "Lost in Translation," "Taxi Driver."

Genres: Thriller, Adventure, Drama, Comedy, Film Noir.

Personal Experiences: Think about moments in your life that have had a significant impact on you, such as a memorable trip, a challenging period, or a unique encounter.

Why These Inspire You: Write down what specifically about these directors, films, or genres inspires you. Is it the storytelling, the visual style, the emotional impact, or something else?

Watch and Learn: Create a watchlist of influential films across different genres. Websites like IMDb's Top 250 or The Criterion Collection can provide excellent recommendations.

Developing Your Story

Once an idea strikes, the next step is to develop it into a cohesive story. This process can be both exhilarating and challenging. My first short film, "Faithless," was born from an idea I encountered while reading another short script. I was so captivated by the potential of the story world that I approached the writer and proposed expanding it into a larger narrative. Thankfully, the writer agreed, and "Faithless" came to life.

Renowned director Christopher Nolan advises, "Every film should have its own world, a logic and feel to it that expands beyond the exact image that the audience is seeing." Developing your story means creating a world with its own rules, characters, and conflicts.

Tips for Developing Your Story

Start Small: Begin with a simple premise and expand upon it. Ask yourself "What if?" questions to delve deeper into your idea. For instance, "What if a detective had to solve a crime in a dream world?" led to Nolan's "Inception."

Create Characters with Depth: Ensure your characters have distinct personalities, backgrounds, and motivations. This will make them more relatable and engaging.

Set Clear Stakes: What does your protagonist stand to lose or gain? Clear stakes will drive your story forward.

Exercise: Brainstorming Session
Mind Mapping:

Start with your core idea in the centre.

Branch out with sub-ideas related to characters, settings, conflicts, and themes.

Example: If your core idea is a mystery set in a small town, branch out to include characters like the detective, suspects, and witnesses.

What If…? Ask yourself "What if?" questions to expand your idea.

Example: What if the protagonist discovers a hidden talent? What if the antagonist has a sympathetic backstory?

Tools and Resources:
Use online mind mapping tools like MindMeister or Miro. Refer to books like "Save the Cat! Writes a Novel" by Jessica Brody for structuring ideas.

Structuring Your Story
Ideas are plentiful, but structuring them into an engaging format is where the real work begins. One common challenge is ensuring that the story is compelling enough for the audience to care about the characters. Do they have enough depth? Are their motivations clear?

Quotes and Insights
To ensure your structure is solid, consider insights from industry experts. Syd Field, author of "Screenplay: The Foundations of Screenwriting," emphasizes the importance of the three-act structure: "The paradigm is a form, not a formula; it serves as a guide, not a rule."

Tips for Structuring Your Story
Three-Act Structure: Divide your story into three acts – Setup, Confrontation, and Resolution. This classic structure helps in creating a well-paced narrative.

Act 1: Setup: Introduce your characters, setting, and the central conflict.

Act 2: Confrontation: Develop the conflict, show the protagonist's struggles.

Act 3: Resolution: Bring the story to a climax and resolve the conflict.

Character Arcs: Ensure your characters undergo significant development. They should change as a result of the events in the story.

Conflict: Introduce a central conflict that drives the story. It can be internal (within the character) or external (against other characters or forces).

Exercise: Outline Your Story
Act 1: Setup:

Introduce your main characters and their world.

Establish the central conflict.

Example: In a mystery, this might be the discovery of a crime.

Act 2: Confrontation:

Develop the conflict through a series of escalating events.

Show how your characters deal with these challenges.

Example: The detective faces obstacles and uncovers clues.

Act 3: Resolution:

Bring the story to its climax.

Resolve the central conflict and show the outcomes for the characters.

Example: The detective solves the mystery, and justice is served.

Watching and Learning

To develop your unique voice in filmmaking, immerse yourself in a wide variety of films. Watch movies across different genres, paying attention to both what works and what doesn't. Bad movies, in particular, can be valuable learning tools, highlighting pitfalls to avoid.

Exercise: Film Analysis

Watch a Film:

Choose a film you admire and one you think failed. Take notes on what you like and dislike.

Example: Compare "Jaws" for its tension and pacing with a less successful film for its flaws.

Analyse Scenes:
Focus on specific scenes. How are they shot? What makes them effective or ineffective?

Example: Analyse the beach scene in "Jaws" for its use of suspense and editing.

Apply Lessons:
Think about how you can apply these lessons to your own project.

Example: Use suspense techniques from "Jaws" to create tension in your own story.

Visualising Your Story

One effective technique for visualising your story is to use stills from other movies. These images can help you conceptualise tone, theme, and shot composition, even if they come from different genres or styles.

Websites like ShotDeck provide a vast database of stills from various films, which can be invaluable for your visual planning.

Exercise: Create a Visual Mood Board
Collect Stills:

Gather stills from films that resonate with the story you want to tell. Look for images that capture the essence of your narrative.

Example: Use stills from "Vertigo" for tension, "Lost in Translation" for mood.

Organise Them:
Arrange these stills on a board (physical or digital) to create a visual reference for your film's aesthetic.

Example: Use Pinterest or a physical corkboard.

Analyse:
Examine how these images reflect your story's tone, theme, and visual style. Use them to guide your creative decisions.

Example: Note the use of lighting in stills from "Blade Runner" to influence your film noir project.

Tools and Resources:
ShotDeck for high-quality film stills.

Books like "The Visual Story" by Bruce Block for understanding visual components.

Conclusion
Finding and developing an idea for your short film is a journey of exploration and discovery. It involves drawing inspiration from various sources, structuring your narrative thoughtfully, learning from a diverse range of films, and visualising your story effectively. Embrace this creative process with enthusiasm, and remember that every great film starts with a spark of an idea. Welcome to the beginning of your filmmaking journey. Let's transform that spark into a captivating story ready to be brought to life on screen.

Chapter 2: Scriptwriting for Short Films

Basics of Screenwriting

Screenwriting is the art of crafting a story specifically for the screen. It's about visual storytelling and creating a script that can guide directors, actors, and crew in bringing a film to life. A well-written script is the backbone of any successful film. Understanding the basics of screenwriting is essential for any aspiring filmmaker.

Key Elements of a Script

Format: Screenplays have a unique format. They include scene headings, action lines, character names, dialogue, and parentheticals.

Structure: Most screenplays follow a three-act structure – setup, confrontation, and resolution.

Show, Don't Tell: Visual storytelling is about showing the audience rather than telling them. Use action and dialogue to reveal character and plot.

Brevity: Screenwriting is about being concise. Every word should serve a purpose.

Tools and Software

Final Draft: Industry-standard software for scriptwriting.

Celtx: A versatile and user-friendly option for beginners.

WriterDuet: Great for collaborative writing.

Structure of a Short Film Script

Short films typically range from 5 to 20 minutes, so your script needs to be concise yet impactful. The structure of a short film script follows the same principles as a feature film but in a condensed format.

Act 1: Setup:

Introduce characters, setting, and the main conflict.

Example: In "The Present," a boy receives a gift that changes his perspective.

Act 2: Confrontation:

Develop the conflict and characters.

Example: The boy struggles to accept the gift due to his own insecurities.

Act 3: Resolution:

Resolve the conflict, showing character growth or change.

Example: The boy learns to embrace the gift, leading to a heart-warming conclusion.

Exercise: Writing Your First Draft

Outline: Create a detailed outline of your story, breaking it into three acts.

Scene List: Write a list of scenes, detailing what happens in each one.

First Draft: Using your outline and scene list, write the first draft of your script.

Writing Engaging Characters and Dialogue

Characters and dialogue are crucial elements of a screenplay. Well-developed characters and natural-sounding dialogue can make your story more engaging and relatable.

Tips for Character Development
Backstory: Give your characters a backstory that informs their actions and decisions.

Motivations: Understand what drives your characters. What do they want, and why?

Flaws and Strengths: Characters should have both flaws and strengths to make them relatable.

Tips for Writing Dialogue
Natural Speech: Write dialogue that sounds natural and reflects how people speak.

Subtext: Use subtext to add depth. Characters don't always say what they mean.

Purpose: Ensure every line of dialogue serves a purpose, either advancing the plot or revealing character.

Exercise: Character and Dialogue
Character Bios: Write a biography for each of your main characters. Include their backstory, motivations, strengths, and flaws.

Dialogue Practice: Write a scene focusing on dialogue between two characters. Ensure the conversation reveals something about their relationship or advances the plot.

Formatting Your Script

Proper formatting is crucial in screenwriting. A well-formatted script shows professionalism and makes it easier for others to read and understand your story.

Elements of Script Formatting

Scene Headings: Indicate the location and time of day (e.g., INT. HOUSE - DAY).

Action Lines: Describe the action and setting.

Character Names: Centred and capitalized when they first appear.

Dialogue: Centred and indented, under the character's name.

Parentheticals: Brief instructions on how a line should be delivered.

Tools and Resources
Screenwriting Software: Use tools like Final Draft or Celtx to ensure your script is properly formatted.

Script Samples: Read sample scripts from websites like IMSDB or SimplyScripts to understand professional formatting.

Exercise: Formatting Practice
Download a Template: Use a screenwriting template from Final Draft or Celtx.

Reformat a Scene: Take a scene from a favourite film and reformat it using the template.

Review: Compare your formatted scene with the original to ensure accuracy.

Collaborating with Writers and Networking
Collaboration can enhance your script by bringing in fresh perspectives. Networking with writers can lead to fruitful partnerships and better stories.

Finding Scripts Written by Other Writers
Online Script Libraries and Marketplaces: Websites like SimplyScripts, Script Reader Pro, and The Black List.

Film Schools and Writing Programs: Connect with students and alumni from film schools. Attend scriptwriting workshops and seminars.

Screenwriting Competitions and Festivals: Participate in screenplay competitions and leverage festival networks to discover emerging writers.

Social Media and Online Communities: Use platforms like LinkedIn, Facebook groups (e.g., "Screenwriting" or "Film and TV Production Crew"), and Reddit communities like r/Screenwriting.

Engaging with Writers

Crafting Your Initial Outreach: Write a compelling and respectful introduction. Highlight your passion for filmmaking and your vision. Provide examples of your work or concept to build credibility.

Starting a Dialogue: Ask thoughtful questions about their script and writing process. Express genuine interest and provide constructive feedback.

Negotiating Collaborations: Discuss terms of collaboration upfront. Set clear expectations and roles. Draft a collaboration agreement to formalize the partnership.

Networking and Marketing Yourself as a Serious Filmmaker

Building Your Personal Brand: Craft a professional online presence. Create a filmmaker's website and portfolio. Utilize social media to showcase your work and connect with industry professionals.

Effective Networking Strategies: Attend industry events and film festivals. Leverage alumni networks and industry connections. Consistently follow up and maintain relationships.

Presenting Yourself Professionally: Prepare a polished elevator pitch. Create a compelling resume and cover letter tailored to the film industry. Develop a strong, visual pitch deck for your film projects.

Marketing Your Work: Utilize social media and digital marketing strategies. Create engaging content around your projects (e.g., behind-the-scenes footage, director's commentary). Build a mailing list and engage with your audience regularly.

Seeking Mentorship and Guidance: Identify potential mentors in the industry. Approach experienced filmmakers for advice and support. Participate in mentorship programs and workshops.

Exercise: Reaching Out to a Writer
Choose a Script: Select a script from an online library or a writer you found through networking.

Draft an Email: Write a respectful and engaging email introducing yourself and expressing interest in their work. Outline your vision and how you see a potential collaboration.

Follow Up: Send the email and follow up after a week if you don't hear back. Be polite and persistent.

Successful Collaborations
One of my most rewarding experiences was collaborating with a writer on "Faithless." The initial idea came from a

script I read, and I was so captivated that I reached out to the writer. This collaboration expanded the story into a rich narrative that won awards at film festivals. Engaging with others in the industry can open doors to incredible opportunities and creative growth.

Conclusion
Scriptwriting is a fundamental skill for any filmmaker. It requires a solid understanding of structure, engaging characters, and well-crafted dialogue. Collaborating with writers and building a network can further enhance your storytelling capabilities. Use the exercises and resources provided to develop your scriptwriting skills and prepare for the next steps in your filmmaking journey.

Chapter 3: Pre-Production Planning

Importance of Pre-Production

Pre-production is a vital phase where you lay the groundwork for your film. It involves fleshing out ideas, planning logistics, and setting up a smooth shoot. Thorough pre-production can save money, avoid pitfalls, and ensure a more enjoyable filmmaking experience.

Key Elements of Pre-Production

Script Breakdown: Identifying all elements required for production, such as props, costumes, locations, and special effects.

Budgeting: Creating a detailed budget outlining all projected costs.

Casting: Finding the right actors to bring your characters to life.

Location Scouting: Securing locations that fit the vision of your film.

Scheduling: Developing a production schedule for efficient time and resource management.

Script Breakdown: What It Is and How to Do It

Script breakdown is the process of analysing your script to identify all necessary elements for production. This ensures thorough planning and prevents any elements from being overlooked.

Why It's Done

Organization: Helps organize all aspects of the production.

Budgeting: Identifies needed elements for accurate budgeting.

Scheduling: Ensures efficient scheduling by knowing what is needed for each scene.

Resource Management: Helps manage resources and personnel effectively.

How to Do a Script Breakdown

Print the Script: Print a hard copy of your script for easier markup.

Get Coloured Pens: Use different coloured pens or highlighters to mark different elements (e.g., red for props, blue for costumes).

Read Through the Script: Do an initial read-through to understand the story's flow and requirements.

Highlight Elements: Line by line, highlight the following:
Props: Objects actors use or interact with.
Cast: All speaking and non-speaking characters.
Costumes: Specific clothing or accessories for characters.
Set Dressing: Items that create the environment but aren't used by actors.
VFX/SFX: Any special or visual effects required.
Stunts: Any physical actions requiring special coordination.
Locations: Different settings for the scenes.

Create a Breakdown Sheet: Transfer highlighted information to a breakdown sheet, either manually or using software like StudioBinder or Movie Magic Scheduling.

Example Breakdown
Scene 1:

Props: Coffee cup, newspaper.

Cast: John (Main Character), Mary (Supporting Character).

Costumes: John's business suit, Mary's casual outfit.

Set Dressing: Office desk, computer, potted plant.

Location: Office interior.

VFX: None.

SFX: Telephone ringing.

Scene 2:

Props: Flashlight, map.

Cast: John, Mary, Security Guard (Minor Character).

Costumes: John's casual clothes, Mary's outdoor gear, Security Guard's uniform.

Set Dressing: Warehouse shelves, crates, forklift.

Location: Warehouse interior.

VFX: Flashlight beam effects.

SFX: Footsteps echoing, door creaking.

Tools and Resources

StudioBinder: Comprehensive tools for script breakdowns and production management.

Movie Magic Scheduling: Industry-standard software for scheduling and breakdowns.

Books: "Script Supervising and Film Continuity" by Pat P. Miller for deeper insights into script breakdown and continuity.

Budgeting: Creating a Detailed Budget

Creating a detailed budget is crucial for managing finances throughout the production. It helps allocate funds efficiently and prepare for unexpected expenses.

Steps for Budgeting

Estimate Costs: Break down your budget into categories such as pre-production, production, post-production, and marketing. Use templates from resources like Film Budgeteers for guidance.

Plan for Contingencies: Include a contingency fund (typically 10-15% of your budget) to cover unexpected expenses.

Track Expenses: Use budgeting software or spreadsheets to track your expenses and stay within budget.

Exercise: Draft a Basic Budget

Create a Budget Template: Use online resources to find a suitable budget template.

Estimate Costs: Fill in estimated costs for each category, considering all aspects of your production.

Review and Adjust: Regularly review your budget and adjust as necessary to stay on track.

Assembling Your Team: Roles and Responsibilities

Your film's success heavily depends on the team you assemble. Each member plays a vital role in bringing your vision to life. Understanding these roles and finding the right people for each position is crucial. Whilst the list isn't exhaustive, for a small dynamic shoot, these initial hires will get you to a good place to film.

Key Roles in a Film Production

Producer: Manages the overall production, including financing, hiring key personnel, and overseeing production logistics.

Director: Leads the creative aspects of the film, including directing actors and making crucial decisions about the film's visual and narrative style.

Director of Photography (DP): Oversees the visual aspects of the film, including camera work and lighting.

Assistant Director (AD): Manages the shooting schedule and coordinates the activities on set.

Production Designer: Creates the visual concept of the film, including sets, locations, and costumes.

Sound Engineer: Manages all aspects of sound recording and mixing.

Finding Collaborators and Crew

Networking: Attend film festivals, workshops, and industry events to meet potential collaborators.

Online Platforms: Use websites like [Mandy](), [ProductionHub](), and [Stage 32]() to find crew members.

Film Schools: Connect with students and alumni from local film schools who are often eager to gain experience.

Exercise: Assembling Your Team

Identify Key Roles: List the key roles you need to fill for your production.

Create Job Descriptions: Write clear job descriptions for each role, outlining responsibilities and requirements.

Network and Recruit: Use networking events, online platforms, and local film schools to find potential team members. Draft and send out recruitment messages.

Casting: Finding the Right Actors

Casting is one of the most critical aspects of pre-production. The right actors can bring your characters to life and elevate your story. Casting involves auditions, call-backs, and negotiations to secure the best talent for your film.

Steps for Successful Casting

Casting Breakdown: Create a detailed casting breakdown that outlines the characteristics and requirements for each role.

Auditions: Hold auditions to evaluate actors' suitability for the roles. Use casting calls on platforms like Backstage and Casting Networks.

Call backs: Invite shortlisted actors for call backs to see how they perform in different scenes and with other actors.

Negotiations: Once you have selected your actors, negotiate terms and contracts.

Exercise: Casting Your Film

Create a Casting Breakdown: Write a detailed description for each character, including age, appearance, personality traits, and any special skills required.

Plan Auditions: Set up audition dates and prepare scenes for actors to perform. Use online platforms to announce your casting call.

Conduct Auditions: Evaluate actors based on their performance, suitability for the role, and chemistry with other actors.

Location Scouting and Set Preparation

Locations play a significant role in setting the tone and atmosphere of your film. Finding the right locations requires careful planning and scouting.

Steps for Location Scouting

Identify Needs: Determine what locations are needed based on your script. Consider practical aspects like accessibility, permissions, and costs.

Scout Locations: Visit potential locations to assess their suitability. Take photos and notes to compare options.

Secure Permits: Obtain necessary permits and permissions from local authorities or property owners.

Prepare the Set: Ensure the location is ready for filming. This may involve set dressing, securing necessary equipment, and coordinating logistics.

Exercise: Scout and Select Locations

List Location Requirements: Write down the specific requirements for each location needed in your script.

Research and Visit: Research potential locations online and visit them to assess their suitability. Take detailed notes and photos.

Obtain Permits: Contact local authorities or property owners to secure permits and permissions.

Scheduling: Creating a Production Schedule

A production schedule ensures that all aspects of your film are coordinated and that everyone knows what needs to be done and when.

Steps for Creating a Production Schedule

Break Down the Script: Identify all scenes, locations, and elements required for each shoot day.

Plan the Shoot: Determine the most efficient order for shooting scenes, considering factors like location availability and actor schedules.

Create a Schedule: Use tools like StudioBinder to create a detailed production schedule.

Communicate the Schedule: Ensure all cast and crew members have access to the schedule and understand their responsibilities.

Exercise: Create a Production Schedule

Break Down Your Script:

List all scenes in the order they appear.

Identify the elements needed for each scene (cast, props, locations, special effects, etc.).

Example: Scene 1 requires John (Main Character), coffee cup (prop), office setting (location).

Draft a Schedule:

Create a calendar or timeline for your shoot.

Allocate specific dates for each scene, considering the availability of locations and actors.

Example: Scene 1 will be shot on Monday, utilizing the office setting and actor availability.

Review and Finalize:
Discuss the draft schedule with your key team members (Producer, AD, DP).
Make necessary adjustments based on feedback and constraints.
Finalize the schedule and distribute it to all cast and crew members.

Assembling Your Team: Roles and Responsibilities
Your film's success heavily depends on the team you assemble. Each member plays a vital role in bringing your vision to life. Understanding these roles and finding the right people for each position is crucial.

Conclusion
Pre-production is a vital phase that sets the foundation for your film's success. By thoroughly planning and organizing each aspect, from budgeting and casting to location scouting

and scheduling, you can ensure a smoother production process. Use the exercises and resources provided to develop a comprehensive pre-production plan and prepare for the next steps in your filmmaking journey.

Pre-production is a complex and detailed phase that requires meticulous planning and organization. By breaking down your script, creating a detailed budget, assembling a reliable team, casting the right actors, and scouting suitable locations, you set a solid foundation for your film. With the exercises and tools provided in this chapter, you're well-equipped to tackle the pre-production process and move closer to bringing your film to life.

Chapter 4: Storyboarding and Shot Planning

Importance of Visualizing Your Film

Storyboarding and shot planning are crucial steps in the pre-production process. They allow you to visualize your film before you start shooting, ensuring that you have a clear idea of what each scene will look like and how the story will flow. This preparation can save time and money during production and help communicate your vision to your cast and crew.

Storyboarding involves creating a sequence of drawings that represent each shot in your film. These drawings help you plan the composition, camera angles, and movement for each scene. Shot planning, on the other hand, involves creating a detailed plan for each shot, including the camera setup, lighting, and blocking of actors.

Creating Storyboards
Storyboards are visual representations of your script. They don't need to be detailed or artistically perfect; simple

sketches are often enough. The key is to capture the essential elements of each shot.

Steps to Create Storyboards

Read the Script: Familiarise yourself with the script and visualize how each scene will look.

Create a Shot List: List all the shots you need for each scene, including details like camera angles, movements, and transitions.

Sketch the Shots: Draw simple sketches of each shot. Include key details like character positions, props, and background elements.

Add Annotations: Write notes on each storyboard frame to describe the action, dialogue, and any special effects or camera movements.

Tools and Resources

Storyboard Templates: Use templates from websites like StudioBinder or Boords.

Storyboard Software: Tools like Storyboard That and ShotPro can help you create digital storyboards.

Example Storyboard

Scene 1:

Shot 1: Wide shot of the office exterior. Annotation: Establishing shot, early morning.

Shot 2: Medium shot of John entering the office. Annotation: John looks determined.

Shot 3: Close-up of John's face. Annotation: John notices something unusual on his desk.

Shot 4: Over-the-shoulder shot of John looking at a mysterious envelope on his desk. Annotation: Focus on the envelope, creating suspense.

Key Terminology for Shot Types:
Wide Shot (WS): Captures the entire scene, establishing the location.

Medium Shot (MS): Shows the character from the waist up, focusing on action.

Close-Up (CU): Focuses on the character's face, capturing emotions.

Exercise: Create Your Own Storyboard

Select a Scene: Choose a scene from your script to storyboard.

List Shots: Create a shot list for the scene, detailing camera angles and movements.

Draw Storyboards: Sketch each shot and add annotations.

Shot Planning

Shot planning involves detailing every aspect of each shot in your film. This includes the camera setup, lighting, blocking of actors, and any special effects. Detailed shot planning ensures that you are prepared for each shoot day and can work efficiently on set.

Steps to Plan Shots

Create a Shot List: List all the shots for each scene, including shot types, angles, and movements.

Determine Camera Setup: Plan the camera positions and movements for each shot.

Plan Lighting: Decide on the lighting setup for each shot, considering the mood and tone of the scene.

Block Actors: Plan the movements and positions of actors within each shot.

Include Special Effects: Detail any special effects or props needed for each shot.

Tools and Resources

Shot List Templates: Use templates from websites like StudioBinder or FilmDirecting.com.

Shot Planning Software: Tools like Shot Lister and Celtx can help you create detailed shot plans.

Example Shot Plan

Here is an example of a shot list in a spreadsheet format:

Scene	Shot #	Description	Shot Type	Camera Setup	Lighting	Blocking	Special Effects
1	1	Office exterior	WS	Static on tripod	Natural light	No actors	None
1	2	John entering office	MS	Dolly following	Overhead fluorescent	John walks to desk	None
1	3	John's face	CU	Static on tripod	Key light on face	John at desk	None

Exercise: Plan Shots for a Scene

Select a Scene: Choose a scene from your script to plan shots for.

Create a Shot List: List all the shots needed for the scene, including details like shot types and camera movements.

Plan Each Shot: Detail the camera setup, lighting, blocking, and any special effects for each shot.

Conclusion

Storyboarding and shot planning are essential steps in the pre-production process that help you visualize your film and ensure that you are prepared for each shoot day. By creating detailed storyboards and shot plans, you can communicate your vision to your cast and crew, save time and money during production, and create a more cohesive and visually compelling film.

Through the exercises provided, you can practice creating your own storyboards and shot plans, ensuring that you are well-prepared for the production phase of your film. By investing time and effort into these pre-production tasks, you set yourself up for a successful and efficient shoot, bringing your vision to life on screen.

Chapter 5: Location Scouting and Set Preparation

Importance of Location Scouting

Choosing the right location for your film is crucial in setting the tone, atmosphere, and authenticity of your story. A well-scouted location can add depth and realism to your film, whereas an unsuitable location can detract from the narrative and distract the audience. Location scouting involves finding, evaluating, and securing locations that match the vision and requirements of your script.

Benefits of Location Scouting

Visual Consistency: Ensures the visual style and atmosphere align with the story.

Practicality: Confirms that the location can accommodate the technical and logistical needs of the production.

Cost Efficiency: Helps in negotiating and securing locations within the budget.

Steps for Effective Location Scouting

Read the Script Thoroughly

Understand the specific needs for each scene, including time of day, setting, and specific visual elements.

Create a Location Breakdown
List all the locations needed for the film, including interior and exterior settings.

Research Potential Locations
Use online resources, local knowledge, and location libraries to find potential sites. Websites like LocationWorks and FilmLocations.com can be helpful.

Assessing Locations for Suitability
When visiting potential locations, consider the following factors:

Budget: Is the location within your budget? Consider costs for renting the space, permits, and any additional fees.

Availability: Ensure the location is available during your shooting schedule.

Logistics: Can the location accommodate the size of your crew and equipment?

Green Rooms: Is there space for actors to rest and prepare?

Crew Workstations: Is there enough space for production offices, equipment storage, and other work areas?

Facilities: Are there sufficient restrooms for the cast and crew?

Noise Levels: Assess ambient noise levels. Can noisy equipment be turned off during filming?

Lighting Conditions: Evaluate natural lighting and whether additional lighting equipment is needed.

Power Supply: Is there adequate power for your equipment? If not, can generators be used?

Safety: Ensure the location is safe for cast and crew, with no hazardous conditions.

Take Photos and Notes
Document each location with photos and detailed notes to help make informed decisions later.

Get Permissions and Permits
Once a location is chosen, secure the necessary permissions and permits from property owners or local authorities.

Plan for Logistics
Ensure the location can support your production needs, including parking, restrooms, and areas for cast and crew to rest.

Exercise: Location Breakdown and Scouting
Create a Location Breakdown: List all the locations required for your script.

Research Potential Locations: Use online tools and local resources to find at least three potential locations for each setting.

Visit Locations: Schedule visits to assess suitability. Take detailed photos and notes for comparison.

Engaging with Professional Location Scouts
Professional location scouts have extensive networks and knowledge that can help find the perfect locations for your film. Websites like Giggster and Peerspace provide platforms to connect with location scouts and explore a variety of filming locations.

How to Engage with Location Scouts

Research and Contact: Look for location scouts in your area through online directories or film commission websites.

Prepare a Brief: Create a detailed brief of your location requirements, including the type of setting, specific features needed, budget, and schedule.

Set Up Meetings: Arrange meetings or calls to discuss your project in detail.

Visit Locations: Accompany the scout to potential locations and assess their suitability together.

Negotiate Fees: Discuss and agree on the scout's fees and any additional costs.

Preparing the Set

Once locations are secured, the next step is set preparation. This involves transforming the location to match the vision of your script, including set dressing, arranging props, and ensuring the environment is safe and functional for filming.

Steps for Set Preparation

Design the Set: Work with your production designer to plan the layout and look of each set. Consider the aesthetic and practical requirements.

Set Dressing: Arrange furniture, props, and decorations to create the desired look and feel.

Lighting Setup: Plan and install the lighting to achieve the necessary visual effects and mood.

Sound Preparation: Ensure the location is suitable for sound recording. Address any issues with background noise or acoustics.

Safety Checks: Conduct a thorough safety inspection to ensure the set is safe for cast and crew. This includes checking for hazards, securing loose equipment, and having emergency procedures in place.

Rehearsals: Conduct rehearsals with the cast and crew to ensure everyone is familiar with the set and can move smoothly during filming.

Exercise: Set Design and Preparation

Sketch Set Designs: Create sketches or digital renderings of the set layout.

Set Dressing Plan: List all the props and decorations needed for each set. Arrange them in the planned layout.

Safety Checklist: Develop a checklist to ensure the set is safe and ready for filming.

Safety Checklist

Developing a safety checklist is crucial to ensure the set is safe for all cast and crew members.

Steps:

Identify Hazards: Walk through the set and identify potential hazards, such as loose cables, sharp objects, or unstable structures.

Create the Checklist: Use templates from sites like [Film Safety Guide](#) to develop a comprehensive checklist.

Conduct Safety Meetings: Hold safety meetings with your crew to review the checklist and ensure everyone is aware of safety protocols.

Things to Look Out For:

Ensure fire exits are clear and accessible.

Verify that all electrical equipment is properly installed and grounded.

Have first aid kits and fire extinguishers readily available.

Resources for Further Assistance:

StudioBinder's Guide to Set Safety

[Production Safety Guidelines](#)

By following these steps and using the recommended tools and resources, you can effectively plan and prepare your set, ensuring it is both visually appealing and safe for your cast and crew.

Conclusion

Location scouting and set preparation are critical steps in the pre-production process that ensure your film's visual and logistical needs are met. By thoroughly scouting locations and preparing your sets, you can create a believable and engaging environment for your story.

Use the exercises and tools provided to plan and execute your location scouting and set preparation effectively, setting the stage for a successful production.

Chapter 6: Budgeting and Funding Your Film

Importance of Budgeting and Funding

Creating a detailed budget and securing funding are critical steps in pre-production. A well-planned budget ensures you have the resources to complete your film without financial strain, while effective funding strategies help you secure the necessary capital.

Steps for Creating a Detailed Budget

Identify Categories: Break down your budget into categories such as pre-production, production, post-production, marketing, and contingency.

Estimate Costs: Research and estimate costs for each category. Use online resources and industry standards to guide your estimates. Websites like FilmBudgeteers and The Budget Book provide templates and tools.

Create a Budget Template: Use budgeting software or spreadsheets to create a detailed budget template. Tools like Movie Magic Budgeting and StudioBinder are industry standards.

Track Expenses: Implement a system for tracking expenses throughout the production. Use software or apps to monitor spending and stay within budget.

Example Top Line Budget Categories and Estimates

Category	Description	Estimated Cost
Pre-Production	Script development, location scouting, casting	$5,000
Production	Equipment rental, crew salaries, set design	$50,000
Post-Production	Editing, sound design, VFX	$20,000
Marketing	Advertising, festival submissions	$10,000
Contingency	Unexpected expenses	$10,000
	Total	$95,000

Budgeting: Above and Below the Line

In film budgeting, costs are categorised as "Above the Line" and "Below the Line." This distinction helps manage and allocate the budget effectively.

Above the Line

Definition: Costs associated with major creative talent and decision-makers.

Includes:

Producers: Fees for the film's producers.

Director: Salary for the director.

Screenwriter: Payment for the screenplay.

Principal Cast: Salaries for leading actors and key talent.

Example: If a film has a budget of $1 million, the above-the-line costs might include $200,000 for the director, $150,000 for the screenwriter, and $350,000 for the principal cast.

Below the Line

Definition: Costs associated with the physical production of the film.

Includes:

Crew: Wages for the technical crew (e.g., cinematographers, grips, sound technicians).

Equipment: Rental fees for cameras, lights, and other gear.

Sets and Locations: Costs for set construction, location fees, and permits.

Post-Production: Editing, sound mixing, visual effects, and colour correction.

Miscellaneous: Transportation, catering, and insurance.

Example: In the same $1 million budget, below-the-line costs might include $100,000 for equipment rental, $200,000 for crew salaries, $50,000 for location fees, and $100,000 for post-production.

Example Budget

For a detailed example budget, you can refer to StudioBinder's free film budget template. This template includes a top sheet summary and color-coded sheets for detailed tracking of production expenses.

Additional Resources

For more information on film budgeting, you can visit:

TemplateLab

StudioBinder

No Film School

This separation ensures clarity in budgeting, helping producers allocate resources efficiently and track spending accurately throughout the production process.

Exercise: Draft a Basic Budget

Create a Budget Template: Use online resources to find a suitable budget template.

Estimate Costs: Fill in estimated costs for each category, considering all aspects of your production.

Review and Adjust: Regularly review your budget and adjust as necessary to stay on track.

Funding Your Film

Securing funding is a crucial aspect of pre-production. There are various methods to fund your film, including personal savings, crowdfunding, grants, and investors.

Methods of Funding

Personal Savings: Use your own funds to finance the film. This provides complete control but can be financially risky.

Crowdfunding: Platforms like Kickstarter and Indiegogo allow you to raise funds from the public. Create a compelling campaign with a clear pitch, engaging video, and attractive rewards.

Grants and Fellowships: Apply for grants from organizations like Sundance Institute and National Endowment for the Arts.

Investors: Seek investment from private investors or production companies. Prepare a detailed business plan and pitch your film professionally.

Creating a Successful Crowdfunding Campaign

A successful crowdfunding campaign on platforms like Kickstarter involves careful planning and execution. Here are key components:

Compelling Pitch: Clearly articulate your vision and why the project matters.

Engaging Video: A well-produced video can significantly boost your campaign's appeal.

Attractive Rewards: Offer rewards that incentivize backers.

Steps for Crowdfunding Campaign

Choose a Platform: Select a crowdfunding platform that suits your needs.

Create a Campaign: Develop a compelling pitch, including a video, project description, budget breakdown, and rewards.

Promote the Campaign: Use social media, email marketing, and networking to promote your campaign and reach potential backers.

Engage with Backers: Keep your backers updated on the progress of your film and deliver promised rewards.

Example Crowdfunding Campaign Outline

Introduction: Briefly introduce yourself and your project.

The Pitch: Explain the story, vision, and why it's important.

Budget Breakdown: Show where the funds will go.

Rewards: Offer attractive rewards for different contribution levels.

Promotion Plan: Outline how you will promote the campaign.

Exercise: Plan a Crowdfunding Campaign

Choose a Platform: Research and select a crowdfunding platform.

Develop a Pitch: Write a compelling pitch and create a campaign video.

Plan Rewards: List rewards for different contribution levels.

Promote: Create a marketing plan to promote your campaign.

Detailed Steps for a Successful Kickstarter Campaign

Research Successful Campaigns: Look at examples of successfully funded campaigns to understand what works. Examples include Veronica Mars Movie Project and Kung Fury.

Crafting Your Pitch:

Introduction: Start with a compelling hook that grabs attention.

Project Description: Clearly describe your project, its goals, and why it's unique.

Budget Breakdown: Be transparent about how the funds will be used.

Team: Introduce your team and their qualifications.

Timeline: Provide a realistic timeline for production and delivery.

Creating the Pitch Video:

Introduction: Introduce yourself and your project.

Story and Vision: Explain the story, your vision, and why it matters.

Call to Action: Encourage viewers to support and share the campaign.

Production Quality: Ensure the video is well-produced with good audio and visuals.

Reward Ideas:

Digital Copy of the Film: Provide backers with early access to a digital copy.

Behind-the-Scenes Content: Offer exclusive behind-the-scenes videos or photos.

Name in Credits: Include backers' names in the film credits.

Merchandise: Offer branded merchandise like T-shirts or posters.

Signed Script: Provide a signed copy of the script.

Exclusive Q&A: Host a private Q&A session with the cast and crew.

Premiere Tickets: Offer tickets to the film's premiere.

Personalized Thank You Video: Send personalized thank you videos to backers.

Associate Producer Credit: Offer an associate producer credit for high-level backers.

Visit the Set: Provide an opportunity to visit the set during filming.

Example Written Pitch for Campaign Page
Project Title: "The Last Sunrise"

Introduction: Hi, I'm [Your Name], an independent filmmaker with a passion for storytelling. I'm excited to share my latest project, "The Last Sunrise," a gripping short film about love and survival in a post-apocalyptic world.

The Pitch: "The Last Sunrise" tells the story of Emma and Jack, two survivors navigating a world ravaged by a mysterious catastrophe. With limited resources and growing tension, they must find a way to survive and hold on to their humanity.

Why This Story Matters: In a time where hope seems lost, "The Last Sunrise" explores the resilience of the human spirit and the power of love. This film is not just about survival; it's about finding light in the darkest times.

Budget Breakdown: To bring this vision to life, we need your support. Here's how the funds will be used:

Production Costs: $15,000 (Equipment, locations, crew)

Post-Production: $5,000 (Editing, sound design, VFX)

Marketing: $3,000 (Festival submissions, promotional materials)

Contingency: $2,000 (Unexpected expenses)

Rewards: We have some exciting rewards for our backers:

- $10: Digital copy of the film
- $25: Name in the credits + digital copy
- $50: Behind-the-scenes access + previous rewards
- $100: Signed script + previous rewards
- $250: Exclusive Q&A session + previous rewards
- $500: Associate Producer credit + previous rewards
- $1,000: Visit the set + previous rewards

Promotion Plan: We will promote our campaign through social media, email newsletters, and collaborations with influencers in the film community. Your support and sharing can make a huge difference!

To conclude: Thank you for considering supporting "The Last Sunrise." With your help, we can bring this story to life and share a message of hope and resilience. Let's make this journey together!

Conclusion

Budgeting and funding are essential components of film production. By creating a detailed budget and exploring various funding options, you can ensure your project is financially viable. Use the exercises and resources provided to develop a comprehensive budget and funding plan, setting the foundation for a successful production.

This chapter has provided step-by-step instructions and practical examples to help you navigate the complexities of budgeting and funding your film. By following these guidelines, you can secure the necessary resources to bring your vision to life.

Chapter 7: Equipment and Technical Basics

Importance of Understanding Equipment and Technical Know-How

Having a solid grasp of the equipment and technical basics is crucial for any filmmaker. The right tools and knowledge enable you to capture your vision accurately, maintain professional standards, and troubleshoot issues on set.

Essential Equipment for Short Film Production

Camera: Choose a camera that fits your budget and meets your needs. Options range from DSLRs and mirrorless cameras to professional cinema cameras.

Examples: Canon EOS R5, Sony A7S III, Blackmagic Pocket Cinema Camera 6K.

Lenses: Different lenses offer various focal lengths and apertures, affecting the look of your film.

Examples: Prime lenses (50mm, 85mm) for sharp images and shallow depth of field; zoom lenses (24-70mm) for versatility.

Tripod/Stabilization: A sturdy tripod or stabilizer ensures steady shots.

Examples: Manfrotto tripods, DJI Ronin gimbals.

Lighting: Good lighting is essential for quality footage. Basic kits include key lights, fill lights, and backlights.

Examples: Aputure Light Storm, Godox SL60W.

Sound Equipment: High-quality audio equipment is crucial as poor sound can detract from your film.

Examples: Rode NTG4+ shotgun microphone, Zoom H5 recorder.

Editing Software: Choose software that allows for comprehensive editing and post-production.

Examples: Adobe Premiere Pro, Final Cut Pro, DaVinci Resolve.

Camera Types: Strengths and Weaknesses

Camera Type	Strengths	Weaknesses
DSLR	Affordable, interchangeable lenses, good for stills and video	Limited dynamic range, less robust for video
Mirrorless	Compact, lightweight, excellent image quality	Shorter battery life, fewer lens options compared to DSLRs
Cinema Cameras	Superior image quality, high dynamic range, built for video	Expensive, requires more accessories
Action Cameras	Compact, durable, good for POV shots	Limited manual controls, lower image quality
Smartphones	Convenient, readily available, easy to use	Limited lens options, lower quality in low light

Hire Equipment in the UK and US

UK Hire Companies:

VMI.TV

Procam

Hireacamera

US Hire Companies:

BorrowLenses

LensProToGo

ShareGrid

Technical Basics

Camera Settings: Understand ISO, aperture, and shutter speed to control exposure and depth of field.

ISO: Adjusts the camera's sensitivity to light. Higher ISO increases brightness but can add noise.

Aperture (f-stop): Controls the amount of light entering the lens and affects depth of field. Lower f-stop (e.g., f/1.8) creates a shallow depth of field.

Shutter Speed: Determines how long the camera's sensor is exposed to light. Faster speeds (e.g., 1/1000) freeze motion, while slower speeds (e.g., 1/30) create motion blur.

Lighting Techniques: Learn basic lighting setups like three-point lighting to achieve professional results.

Key Light: The main light source.

Fill Light: Reduces shadows created by the key light.

Back Light: Separates the subject from the background.

Sound Recording: Position microphones close to the source and use windshields to minimize noise.

Boom Mic: Ideal for capturing dialogue.

Lapel Mic: Great for interviews and hidden in costumes.

Composition and Framing: Use the rule of thirds, leading lines, and framing to enhance visual storytelling.

Exercise: Equipment Checklist

List Your Equipment Needs: Based on your script, list all necessary equipment.

Research and Budget: Research options within your budget, including rental costs if applicable.

Create a Checklist: Make a checklist to ensure all equipment is acquired and tested before shooting.

Exercise: Camera and Lighting Test

Set Up a Scene: Choose a scene from your script and set up your camera and lighting.

Adjust Settings: Experiment with different ISO, aperture, and shutter speed settings.

Record and Review: Record test footage, review it, and make adjustments as needed.

Conclusion

Understanding equipment and technical basics is vital for producing high-quality films. By mastering these tools and techniques, you can effectively bring your vision to life on screen. Use the exercises and resources provided to build your technical skills and ensure your film's production runs smoothly.

Chapter 8: Directing Your Short Film

Importance of Effective Directing

Directing involves translating your vision onto the screen, guiding actors, and coordinating with the crew to bring the story to life. Effective directing ensures that your film's narrative and visual style are consistent and engaging.

Steps for Successful Directing
- Communicate Your Vision
- Work with Actors
- Collaborate with the Crew

Communicate Your Vision
Script Analysis: Break down the script to understand characters, themes, and key scenes. This involves identifying the core elements of the story and the emotional beats you want to hit.

Example: If a scene involves a character feeling isolated, your direction might focus on using wide shots to emphasize their loneliness.

Storyboards and Shot Lists: Use these tools to visualize scenes and plan shots. Storyboards provide a visual representation of each scene, while shot lists detail the specific shots you need to capture.

Example: Create a storyboard sequence showing how a confrontation scene will unfold, including camera angles and movements.

Look books: Create a visual reference guide that includes images, colour schemes, and textures to communicate your vision to the team. Look books can help align everyone on the aesthetic direction of the film.

Example: A look book for a noir film might include images with high contrast, dark shadows, and urban settings.

Exercise: Develop a Look book
Collect Visual References: Gather images from films, photography, art, and other sources that match your vision.

Organize by Theme: Arrange the images by theme, colour scheme, or scene to create a cohesive look book.

Share with Your Team: Distribute the look book to your crew to ensure everyone understands the visual style.

Working with Actors

Working with actors is one of the most crucial aspects of filmmaking. Actors are the lifeblood of your story, bringing characters to life with depth, emotion, and authenticity. As a director, your role is not to tell actors what to do or say but to create an environment where they can explore and express their characters fully. Understanding what actors do and what they bring to a project can significantly enhance the quality of your film.

Actors are not merely "meat puppets" to be manipulated; they are artists who interpret and embody the characters you have created. They bring their own experiences, emotions, and creativity to the role, adding layers of complexity and realism that enrich your story. Effective collaboration with actors involves clear communication, mutual respect, and a deep understanding of the craft of acting.

The Role of Actors
Actors bring a multitude of skills and qualities to a film, including:
1. **Interpretation**: Actors interpret the script and understand the character's motivations, background, and development.
2. **Emotional Range**: They use their emotional depth to portray a wide range of feelings and reactions, making characters believable and relatable.
3. **Physicality**: Through body language and movement, actors convey aspects of their characters that words alone cannot express.
4. **Collaboration**: Actors work closely with directors and other cast members to ensure that their performances align with the overall vision of the film.

Building a Collaborative Relationship
As a director, building a strong, collaborative relationship with your actors is essential. Here are some key strategies:
1. **Open Communication**: Encourage actors to share their insights and ideas about their characters. Listen

to their suggestions and be open to incorporating their perspectives.
2. **Trust**: Establish trust by respecting their creative process and providing constructive feedback. Trust allows actors to take risks and fully commit to their performances.
3. **Preparation**: Conduct thorough rehearsals to explore different interpretations of scenes and to work out any issues before filming. This preparation helps actors feel more confident and secure in their roles.
4. **Support**: Create a supportive environment on set where actors feel comfortable and valued. Address any concerns they may have and ensure they have the resources they need to perform at their best.

Recommended Reading

To further understand the nuances of working with actors and to refine your directing skills, consider exploring these highly regarded books:

1. **"Directing Actors: Creating Memorable Performances for Film and Television" by Judith Weston**: This book offers practical advice on how to

communicate effectively with actors and create memorable performances.

- https://amzn.to/3yHbZwy

2. **"An Actor Prepares" by Constantin Stanislavski**: A seminal work that delves into the actor's process and the methods used to develop a character.

    - https://amzn.to/4e556oM

3. **"The Art of Acting" by Stella Adler**: This book provides insights into the craft of acting and techniques that can help actors bring their characters to life.

    - https://amzn.to/3R8stUD

4. **"On Directing Film" by David Mamet**: Mamet shares his perspective on directing and offers practical advice for working with actors.

    - https://amzn.to/3KlXa59

5. **"Respect for Acting" by Uta Hagen**: A comprehensive guide that explores the actor's craft

and provides techniques for creating authentic performances.

- <https://amzn.to/3yHl5cA>

By reading these books, you can gain a deeper understanding of the actor's process and learn how to foster a collaborative, creative environment that brings out the best in your actors. Embrace the artistry that actors bring to your project, and your films will be richer and more compelling for it.

Casting: Choose actors who fit the characters and can deliver strong performances. Hold auditions and call backs to find the best fit.

Example: If your character is a troubled teenager, look for actors who can naturally convey vulnerability and intensity.

Rehearsals: Conduct rehearsals to help actors understand their roles and build chemistry. Use this time to experiment with different approaches to scenes.

Example: During rehearsals, run through a pivotal emotional scene multiple times, giving actors different motivations to explore their characters deeply.

On-Set Direction: Provide clear and constructive feedback, and be open to actors' input. Foster a collaborative environment where actors feel comfortable experimenting and suggesting ideas.

Example: If an actor struggles with a line, discuss the character's motivation and try different readings to find what works best.

Exercise: Conduct Effective Rehearsals
Plan Rehearsal Sessions: Schedule time to rehearse key scenes with your actors.
Focus on Character Development: Use rehearsals to explore characters' backstories and motivations.

Experiment with Blocking: Try different movements and interactions to find the most dynamic staging for each scene.

Collaborating with the Crew

Pre-Production Meetings: Hold meetings to ensure everyone understands the vision and plan. Discuss the overall approach, specific scene requirements, and any technical challenges.

Example: In a meeting with your DP and production designer, discuss the visual style and how it will be achieved through lighting and set design.

On-Set Coordination: Maintain open communication with the crew to ensure smooth operations. Be clear about your expectations and be available to answer questions.

Example: During a complex shot, coordinate with the DP, gaffer, and actors to ensure everyone is synchronized.

Problem-Solving: Be prepared to handle unexpected issues that arise on set. Stay calm, assess the situation, and collaborate with your team to find solutions.

Example: If a key prop breaks, work with your production designer to quickly find a replacement or adjust the scene to work without it.

Exercise: Plan Pre-Production Meetings

Schedule Regular Meetings: Set up a schedule for regular pre-production meetings with key department heads.

Create Agendas: Develop agendas for each meeting to ensure all important topics are covered.

Document Decisions: Keep detailed notes of decisions made during meetings to ensure everyone is on the same page.

Case Study: Directing Techniques in "The Shawshank Redemption"

Director: Frank Darabont

Techniques:

Character-Driven Storytelling: Darabont focuses on deep character development, which is evident in the performances of Tim Robbins and Morgan Freeman.

Visual Metaphors: The use of light and shadow throughout the film emphasizes themes of hope and despair.

Example: The final scene, where Andy Dufresne emerges from the sewer into the rain, uses a wide shot to symbolize freedom and rebirth.

Conclusion

Directing is a multifaceted role that requires strong communication, collaboration, and creative vision. By effectively working with actors, collaborating with the crew, and using tools like storyboards and look books, you can bring your film to life in a way that aligns with your artistic vision. Use the exercises and resources provided to hone your directing skills and ensure a successful production.

Chapter 9: Filming Your Short Film

Importance of Efficient Filming

Efficient filming is essential for staying within budget, maintaining morale, and ensuring the quality of your final product. Proper planning and organization can help you maximize your shoot days and capture the footage you need.

On-Set Protocols
Daily Call Sheets: Distribute call sheets daily to inform the cast and crew of the shooting schedule, locations, and any special instructions.

Example Call Sheet Content: Call times, scene numbers, location addresses, contact information, and weather forecasts.

Crew Briefing: Start each day with a briefing to review the day's schedule, discuss potential challenges, and ensure everyone knows their roles.

Example: The director and AD might go over key scenes, while the DP discusses lighting setups.

Maintaining Schedule: Stick to the schedule as closely as possible. Allow time for setup, rehearsals, and breaks.

Tips: Use time management tools like StudioBinder's scheduling software, and keep a visible clock on set.

Efficient Shooting Techniques
Shot Lists and Storyboards: Use shot lists and storyboards to guide your shoot, ensuring you capture all necessary footage.

Example: A storyboard for a dialogue scene might show shot-reverse-shot sequences to cover both actors.

Coverage: Film each scene from multiple angles and distances to provide options in the editing room.

Example: For a dramatic scene, shoot a wide shot for establishing context, medium shots for interactions, and close-ups for emotional intensity.

Blocking and Rehearsals.

Knowing the scenes and rehearsing with actors is essential for planning movements and camera placements to ensure dynamic and coherent shots.

Industry Standard Procedure:

Clear the Floor: The Assistant Director (AD) asks everyone except the key personnel (director, actors) to clear the floor.

Blocking with Actors: The director works with the actors to block the scene, planning out their movements and interactions.

Example: In a chase scene, the director maps out the actors' paths and positions the camera to follow the action fluidly.

Crew Show: Once the director is satisfied with the blocking, the AD calls the crew back on set for the "crew show." During this, the crew observes the blocking to understand their roles and setups.

Adjustments: After the crew show, final adjustments are made to camera positions, lighting, costumes, and set dressing based on the blocking.

Rehearsals: Actors are brought back on set for a rehearsal. This allows everyone to practice and make any further adjustments.

Recording: If the director is happy with the rehearsal, the scene is recorded.

This procedure ensures that every department is in sync and that the scene can be filmed efficiently and effectively.

Handling Technical Issues
Backup Equipment: Always have backup equipment on set, such as spare batteries, memory cards, and cameras.

Example: If a camera malfunctions, having a second camera ready can save valuable time.

Troubleshooting: Be prepared to troubleshoot common issues like audio problems, lighting changes, or equipment failures.

Example: If you encounter unexpected noise, use a boom mic closer to the actor or adjust audio levels in post-production.

Health and Safety on Set
Safety Briefing: Conduct a safety briefing at the start of each shooting day to address potential hazards and emergency procedures.

Example: Discuss fire exits, first aid procedures, and location-specific risks.

Emergency Contacts: Ensure all crew members have a list of emergency contacts and know where the first aid kit is located.

Example: Include emergency contacts on the call sheet and post them visibly on set.

On-Set Medic: Consider having a trained medic on set, especially for shoots with stunts or special effects.

Example: For a film involving fight scenes, a medic can address injuries promptly.

Exercise: Create a Call Sheet

Template: Use a call sheet template from StudioBinder.

Fill in Details: Include call times, scene details, location addresses, crew and cast contact information, and special instructions.

Distribute: Send the call sheet to all cast and crew members at least 12 hours before the shoot.

Case Study: On-Set Efficiency in "Mad Max: Fury Road"

Director: George Miller

Techniques:

Detailed Storyboards: Miller used thousands of storyboard frames to plan the entire film.

Efficient Coverage: Multiple cameras were used to capture high-intensity action scenes from different angles simultaneously.

Example: The chase scenes were meticulously planned and shot with multiple cameras, ensuring dynamic and seamless sequences in the final edit.

Conclusion
Efficient filming practices are crucial for a successful shoot. By adhering to on-set protocols, using efficient shooting techniques, handling technical issues promptly, and ensuring health and safety, you can create a productive and harmonious set environment. Utilize the exercises and case studies provided to refine your filming process and ensure a smooth production.

Chapter 10: Editing Your Short Film

Importance of the Editing Process

Editing is where your film truly comes to life. It involves selecting and combining shots, arranging them in a coherent sequence, and refining the visual and auditory elements to enhance storytelling.

Steps in the Editing Process
Importing Footage

Step-by-Step:

Transfer all your footage from the camera to your computer.

Organize the files into folders by scene or shooting day.
Import the footage into your editing software (e.g., Adobe Premiere Pro, Final Cut Pro, DaVinci Resolve).

Example: Create a folder structure with directories for "Raw Footage," "Scenes," and "Audio Files."

Creating a Rough Cut

The rough cut is your first pass at editing the film. It's about getting all the pieces in place.

Step-by-Step:
Lay out the scenes in the order they appear in the script.
Trim the clips to remove any unusable footage.
Arrange the clips in a sequence that follows the narrative.

Example: Start with the opening scene, place the clips in chronological order, and focus on maintaining the story's flow.

Refining the Edit
This stage involves fine-tuning the timing and transitions to ensure a smooth flow.

Step-by-Step:

Adjust the in and out points of each clip to improve pacing.
Add transitions (e.g., cuts, dissolves) where necessary.
Ensure continuity by matching action and maintaining visual consistency.

Example: If a character walks through a door, make sure the action matches perfectly between the cuts.

Incorporating Sound

Good audio is crucial for a polished final product. This includes dialogue, sound effects, and music.

Step-by-Step:

Sync the audio tracks with the video.

Clean up background noise and adjust levels for clarity.

Add sound effects to enhance the action.

Choose appropriate music that complements the mood and pace of the film.

Example: Use software like Adobe Audition for noise reduction and sound mixing.

Colour Correction and Grading

Colour correction ensures consistency in lighting and colour, while colour grading enhances the visual tone.

Step-by-Step:

Correct any colour imbalances to match the scenes.

Apply colour grading to establish the film's look and feel.

Use tools like DaVinci Resolve for advanced colour grading.

Example: Apply a blue tint for night scenes to create a colder, more dramatic effect.

Adding Titles and Credits
Titles and credits provide essential information and add a professional touch.

Step-by-Step:
Create a title sequence that fits the style of your film.
Add opening credits for key cast and crew members.
Include end credits to acknowledge everyone involved in the production.

Example: Use After Effects to create dynamic titles that match your film's theme.
Final Review and Export
Review the entire film to ensure everything is polished and ready for distribution.

Step-by-Step:

Watch the film from start to finish, making notes on any final tweaks needed.

Adjust any remaining issues with timing, audio levels, or visual elements.

Export the film in the desired format for distribution (e.g., MP4 for online platforms, DCP for cinema screenings).

Example: Export a high-quality master file and create smaller versions for different platforms.

Editing Suites

Choosing the right editing suite can significantly impact the efficiency and quality of your post-production process.

Adobe Premiere Pro: Widely used in the industry, versatile and integrates well with other Adobe products.

Strengths: Robust toolset, frequent updates, extensive support community.

Weaknesses: Subscription-based, can be resource-intensive.

Find It: Adobe Premiere Pro

Final Cut Pro X: Popular among Mac users, known for its intuitive interface and powerful features.

Strengths: Fast performance, magnetic timeline, excellent for Mac integration.

Weaknesses: Mac-only, some initial learning curve.

Find It: Final Cut Pro X

DaVinci Resolve: Renowned for its colour grading capabilities, also a full-featured editing suite.

Strengths: Advanced colour correction, free version available, comprehensive features.

Weaknesses: Can be complex for beginners, requires powerful hardware.

Find It: DaVinci Resolve

Finding Editors

If you prefer to hire an editor, there are several ways to find skilled professionals.

Freelance Websites: Platforms like Upwork, Freelancer, and Fiverr allow you to find freelance editors with various levels of experience and expertise.

Film Schools: Connect with students or recent graduates from film schools. They often seek projects to build their portfolios.

Industry Networks: Use industry networks like Mandy and ProductionHub to find experienced editors.

Post Houses for Short Film Post-Production
Professional post houses can offer high-quality post-production services tailored to short films.

The Mill: Known for its work in visual effects, colour grading, and high-end finishing.

Find It: themill.com

Company 3: Specializes in colour correction and finishing for feature films and shorts.

Find It: company3.com

Deluxe: Provides comprehensive post-production services including editing, colour grading, and sound design.

Find It: bydeluxe.com

ONSIGHT: Known for their valued support at helping short film makers through the post process.

Find It: onsight.co.uk/

Case Study: Editing Techniques in "Mad Max: Fury Road"

Editor: Margaret Sixel

Techniques:

Fast-Paced Editing: Rapid cuts to match the high-intensity action sequences.

Seamless Transitions: Smooth transitions between shots to maintain the film's relentless pace.

Dynamic Sound Design: Integrating sound effects and music to enhance the visceral impact.

Example: In the chase scenes, the editing maintains a frenetic pace, with quick cuts and dynamic angles to heighten tension and excitement.

Conclusion

Editing is a meticulous and creative process that shapes your film into a cohesive and engaging narrative. By following the detailed steps outlined, you can refine your footage into a polished final product. Use the exercises and case studies provided to develop your editing skills and ensure your short film stands out.

Chapter 11: Post-Production Essentials

Importance of Post-Production

Post-production is the phase where your film undergoes final refinements to achieve a polished and professional look. This stage includes colour correction, sound mixing, visual effects, and final mastering, which are crucial for delivering a high-quality film.

Key Elements of Post-Production
Colour Correction and Grading

Sound Mixing

Visual Effects (VFX)

Final Mastering

Colour Correction and Grading
Colour correction ensures consistency in lighting and colour across all scenes, while colour grading enhances the visual tone to match the film's mood and style.

Step-by-Step:

Colour Correction: Adjust exposure, contrast, and white balance to achieve a consistent look.

Example: Use tools in DaVinci Resolve to balance the colours of outdoor and indoor scenes.

Colour Grading: Apply stylistic colour adjustments to enhance the mood.

Example: Add a warm tint to create a nostalgic atmosphere or a cold tint for a dystopian feel.

Tools and Resources:
Software: DaVinci Resolve, Adobe Premiere Pro

Tutorials: Color Grading Central

Sound Mixing
Sound mixing combines all audio elements (dialogue, music, sound effects) into a cohesive soundtrack.

Step-by-Step:

Dialogue Editing: Clean up and balance dialogue tracks.

Example: Use Adobe Audition to remove background noise and enhance vocal clarity.

Sound Effects: Layer sound effects to add depth and realism.

Example: Add ambient sounds like wind or traffic to enhance the setting.

Music Integration: Integrate music seamlessly to support the narrative.

Example: Adjust music levels to ensure it doesn't overpower dialogue.

Tools and Resources:
Software: Pro Tools, Adobe Audition
Libraries: SoundDogs, Freesound

Visual Effects (VFX)
Visual effects add elements that are impractical or impossible to capture during filming.

Step-by-Step:

Identify VFX Shots: List all scenes requiring visual effects.

Example: A scene requiring a digital explosion or a sci-fi landscape.

Plan VFX Workflow: Coordinate with your VFX team to ensure a smooth integration.

Example: Provide the team with necessary footage and references.

Implement and Review: Apply effects and review them for consistency and quality.

Example: Use After Effects to composite layers and add effects.

Tools and Resources:
Software: Adobe After Effects, Nuke, UnrealEngine
Tutorials: Video Copilot, FXhome

Final Mastering
Final mastering prepares your film for distribution by ensuring it meets technical standards.

Step-by-Step:

Final Review: Watch the film in its entirety to catch any remaining issues.
Example: Look for inconsistencies in colour sound levels, and visual effects.
Export Settings: Choose the appropriate settings for your distribution platform.
Example: Export in 4K resolution for theatrical release or 1080p for online platforms.
Quality Check: Perform a quality check to ensure there are no technical glitches.
Example: Use professional monitors and speakers to review the final output.

Tools and Resources:
Software: HandBrake, Compressor
Guidelines: Netflix Partner Help Centre, BBC Technical Standards

Conclusion
Post-production is a critical phase where your film undergoes the final transformations to achieve a polished and professional look. By mastering the key elements of colour correction, sound mixing, VFX, and final mastering,

you can ensure your film meets the highest standards. Utilize the tools, resources, and step-by-step guidelines provided to refine your post-production skills and deliver a standout short film.

Chapter 12: Preparing for the Screening

Importance of a Successful Premiere

The premiere is the first public showing of your film and sets the tone for its reception. A well-planned screening can generate buzz, attract potential distributors, and provide invaluable feedback.

Steps to Prepare for Your Film's Screening
Choose the Right Venue

Plan the Event

Market Your Premiere

Technical Preparation

Engage Your Audience

Choosing the Right Venue
Selecting the appropriate venue is crucial for a successful screening.

Step-by-Step:

Identify Your Audience: Consider who will be attending and choose a venue that suits their expectations.

Example: For industry professionals, choose a reputable cinema or film festival.

Evaluate Venue Options: Visit potential venues to assess their facilities, seating capacity, and screen quality.

Example: Look for venues with high-quality projection and sound systems.

Book Early: Secure your venue well in advance to ensure availability.

Examples of Venues:

Independent Cinemas: Local theatres that support indie films.

Film Festivals: Platforms like Sundance, TIFF, and Cannes.

Community Centres: More intimate settings for smaller audiences.

Plan the Event

Organizing a successful event involves detailed planning and coordination.

Step-by-Step:

Set a Date: Choose a date that allows sufficient time for marketing and preparation.

Send Invitations: Create a guest list and send invitations well in advance.

Example: Use platforms like Eventbrite or Mailchimp for professional invites.

Arrange Catering: If budget allows, provide refreshments or a reception.

Prepare a Schedule: Outline the event's timeline, including introductions, Q&A sessions, and networking opportunities.

Example Schedule:

6:00 PM: Doors open, and guests arrive.

6:30 PM: Screening begins.

8:00 PM: Q&A session with the director and cast.

8:30 PM: Networking reception.

Market Your Premiere
Effective marketing is essential to attract attendees and generate buzz.

Step-by-Step:

Create Promotional Materials: Design posters, flyers, and social media graphics.

Tools: Use Canva or Adobe Spark for easy design creation.

Utilize Social Media: Promote the event on platforms like Facebook, Instagram, and Twitter.

Example: Create an event page on Facebook and share regular updates.

Engage with Local Media: Reach out to local newspapers, radio stations, and bloggers to cover your event.

Email Campaigns: Send newsletters to your mailing list with event details and RSVP links.

Example Campaign:
Subject Line: "Join Us for the Premiere of [Film Title]!"

Content: Brief synopsis of the film, event details, and a call to action to RSVP.

Technical Preparation

Ensure the technical aspects of your screening run smoothly.

Step-by-Step:

Test Equipment: Perform a test run with the venue's projection and sound equipment.

Example: Play the film from start to finish to check for any issues.

Prepare Backup Copies: Have digital and physical copies of the film ready.

Formats: DCP (Digital Cinema Package), Blu-ray, and USB drives.

Coordinate with the Venue: Confirm the venue's technical capabilities and requirements.

Example Checklist:

Test projection quality.

Check audio levels.

Ensure subtitles (if any) are properly displayed.

Engage Your Audience

Interaction with your audience can leave a lasting impression and provide valuable feedback.

Step-by-Step:

Introduction Speech: Prepare a brief speech to introduce the film and thank attendees.

Content: Mention the journey of making the film and acknowledge key contributors.

Q&A Session: Host a Q&A session after the screening to discuss the film with the audience.

Moderator: Have a moderator facilitate the session to keep it engaging.

Feedback Forms: Provide forms or digital surveys for attendees to leave feedback.

Tools: Use Google Forms or SurveyMonkey for online feedback collection.

Example Introduction Speech:

Opening: "Thank you all for coming tonight. It's an honour to share our film with you."

Journey: "This film started as a simple idea and evolved into what you're about to see through the hard work of many talented individuals."

Acknowledgments: "Special thanks to our cast, crew, and everyone who supported us along the way."

Case Study: Successful Premiere of "Moonlight"

Director: Barry Jenkins

Techniques:

Venue Choice: Premiered at the Telluride Film Festival, attracting industry professionals and critics.

Engagement: Barry Jenkins and the cast participated in Q&A sessions, providing insights into the film's creation.

Marketing: Utilized a strong social media presence and targeted press coverage to build anticipation.

Conclusion

Preparing for the screening of your short film involves careful planning, marketing, and technical preparation. By choosing the right venue, organizing a well-structured event, effectively marketing the premiere, ensuring technical readiness, and engaging with your audience, you can create a memorable and impactful screening. Use the detailed steps and case studies provided to guide your preparation and ensure a successful premiere for your film.

Chapter 13: Navigating Film Festivals and Distribution

Importance of Film Festivals and Distribution

Participating in film festivals and effectively distributing your short film can significantly increase its visibility, attract potential distributors, and open doors to new opportunities.

Steps to Submit to Film Festivals
Research and Select Festivals

Prepare Submission Materials

Submit Your Film

Promote Your Screening

Research and Select Festivals
Choosing the right festivals for your film is crucial for maximizing its impact.

Step-by-Step:

Identify Goals: Determine what you want to achieve by entering festivals (e.g., exposure, networking, awards).

Research Festivals: Look for festivals that align with your film's genre, theme, and target audience.

Examples: Sundance, Cannes, Tribeca, TIFF for high-profile exposure; smaller niche festivals for genre-specific audiences.

Check Deadlines and Requirements: Note submission deadlines and specific requirements for each festival.

Resource: Use platforms like FilmFreeway and Withoutabox to find festivals and manage submissions.

Example:

Sundance Film Festival: Known for discovering new talent and showcasing independent films.

Toronto International Film Festival (TIFF): A significant platform for launching films into the North American market.

Prepare Submission Materials
Properly preparing your submission materials increases your chances of acceptance.

Step-by-Step:

Create a Press Kit: Include a synopsis, director's statement, cast and crew bios, and high-quality stills.

Example: A one-page summary highlighting the film's theme, production process, and key contributors.

Prepare a Trailer: Edit a compelling trailer that captures the essence of your film.

Technical Specifications: Ensure your film meets the technical requirements (e.g., format, resolution).

Resource: Refer to each festival's technical specifications page.

Example Press Kit Components:

Synopsis: A brief description of the film's plot and themes.

Director's Statement: Insights into the director's vision and inspiration.

Bios: Short biographies of the key cast and crew.

Stills: High-resolution images from the film.

Submit Your Film

Submitting your film involves following specific guidelines and meeting deadlines.

Step-by-Step:

Register on Submission Platforms: Create profiles on platforms like FilmFreeway and Withoutabox.

Complete Application Forms: Fill out all necessary information accurately.

Upload Materials: Upload your film, press kit, and any additional required materials.

Pay Submission Fees: Ensure you pay the required submission fees to finalize your entry.

Example Platforms:

FilmFreeway

Withoutabox

Promote Your Screening

Promoting your film's screening at festivals can help draw attention and build an audience.

Step-by-Step:

Leverage Social Media: Use social media platforms to announce your festival selection and screening dates.

Example: Create event pages on Facebook and share regular updates on Instagram and Twitter.

Engage with Local Media: Reach out to local newspapers, radio stations, and bloggers for coverage.

Network at the Festival: Attend the festival and network with other filmmakers, distributors, and industry professionals.

Example: Hand out business cards and flyers promoting your screening.

Example Social Media Posts:

Announcement: "Thrilled to announce that [Film Title] will be screening at [Festival Name] on [Date]! Join us for the premiere!"

Behind-the-Scenes: "Getting ready for our big screening at [Festival Name]. Here's a sneak peek behind the scenes!"

Distribution Strategies

After the festival circuit, distributing your film effectively ensures it reaches a broader audience.

Step-by-Step:

Identify Distribution Channels: Choose the best platforms for your film (e.g., online streaming, DVD, theatrical release).

Example: Platforms like Vimeo On Demand and Amazon Prime Video.

Create a Distribution Plan: Outline your strategy, including target audiences, marketing tactics, and release schedule.

Negotiate Distribution Deals: Work with distribution companies to secure deals that benefit your film.

Example: Contact distributors who specialize in short films or your specific genre.

Monitor Performance: Track your film's performance across different platforms and adjust your strategy as needed.

Resources for Distribution:

ShortsTV: A channel dedicated to short films.

Indie Rights: A distributor for independent films.

Conclusion

Navigating film festivals and distribution effectively can significantly enhance the visibility and success of your short film. By carefully selecting festivals, preparing thorough submission materials, promoting your screenings, and developing a strategic distribution plan, you can maximize your film's impact. Use the detailed steps and resources provided to guide your journey through the festival circuit and beyond, ensuring your film reaches its full potential.

Conclusion

Reflecting on Your Journey
As you reach the end of this book, it's important to reflect on the incredible journey you've undertaken. From the initial spark of an idea to the screening of your finished film, you've navigated the complexities of filmmaking with dedication and creativity.

The Importance of Perseverance and Passion
Filmmaking is a challenging but rewarding pursuit. Throughout this journey, perseverance and passion have been your guiding lights. Every setback and triumph has contributed to your growth as a filmmaker. Remember, every great filmmaker has faced obstacles and learned from them.

Encouragement to Continue Making Films
Your first film is just the beginning. Use the skills and knowledge you've gained to continue creating. Each project will bring new challenges and opportunities to improve your craft. Keep pushing boundaries, experimenting with new ideas, and telling stories that matter to you.

Final Anecdote: The Impact of My First Film
I remember the first time my short film "Faithless" was screened. The response was overwhelming, not because it was perfect, but because it resonated with the audience. That experience solidified my love for filmmaking and taught me the power of storytelling. Your journey will have its unique moments of impact—cherish them.

Bonus Section: How to Find Producers for Your Film

Finding the right producer is essential for the success of your film. Producers provide not only financial backing but also organizational skills, industry connections, and creative input that can significantly elevate your project. Here are practical, step-by-step methods for new filmmakers to connect with producers.

Social Media

Social media platforms are powerful tools for networking and finding producers. Here are ways to leverage different social media channels:

1. **Facebook Groups**
   - **Join Local Filmmaking Groups**: Search for filmmaking groups relevant to your location or genre.
   - **Introduce Yourself**: Share a post introducing yourself, the type of films you create, and what you're looking for.
     - **Example Post**: "Hi everybody! I'm a screenwriter and director based in [your town/city] looking to connect

with short film producers. I'm excited to collaborate on my upcoming project and can't wait to meet passionate producers who are interested in working together!"
- ○ **Search for Producers**: Use the group's search function to look for posts mentioning producers.
  - **How to Search**: Click the magnifying glass in the top right corner of the group page and type 'producers'.

2. **Instagram**
   - ○ **Share Your Introduction Post**: Adapt and share your Facebook introduction as a regular post, reel, or story.
   - ○ **Use Relevant Hashtags**: Find and engage with producers using hashtags.
     - **Examples**: #britishfilmproducer, #indiefilmproducer, #shortfilmproducer.
   - ○ **Engage with Content**: Comment on posts from producers and filmmaking

communities to build connections, but don't overdo it. No spamming!

3. **Twitter**
   - **Adapt Your Post for Twitter**: Share a version of your Facebook post as a tweet.
   - **Use Hashtags**: Search and use hashtags to find and engage with producers.
     - **Examples**: #filmproducer, #indiefilm, #shortfilm.
   - **Engage with Content**: Like, retweet, and comment on posts from producers and filmmaking communities.

4. **LinkedIn**
   - **Share Your Post**: Adapt your Facebook post for LinkedIn.
   - **Search for Producers**: Use LinkedIn's search function to find producers in your network or industry.
   - **Connect and Message**: Send connection requests with a personalized message.
     - **Example Message**: "Hi [Name], I'm a filmmaker looking to collaborate with producers for my

next short film. I'd love to connect and discuss potential opportunities."

Educational Institutions

Film schools and educational programs are excellent places to find emerging producers.

1. **Film Schools**
    - **Research Producing Courses**: Look for specific producing courses offered by film schools.
    - **Contact Course Leaders**: Email the course leader or administrator to ask if they can share your information with past and current students.
        - **Example Email**: "Dear [Course Leader], I'm a filmmaker seeking to collaborate with producers. Could you please share my contact details with your producing course students?"
2. **Networking at Film Schools**
    - **Attend School Events**: Participate in film school events, screenings, and workshops to meet producing students and alumni.

- o **Engage with Faculty**: Build relationships with faculty members who can introduce you to promising students.

Online Databases and Industry Resources
Utilize online platforms and databases to find and contact producers.

1. **IMDb**
   - o **Search for Producers**: Use IMDb to find producers of films you love and are influenced by.
   - o **Use IMDb Pro**: Access contact information with an IMDb Pro subscription.
   - o **Reach Out**: Email or message producers, referencing their previous work and your interest in collaborating.
2. **Freelancer Databases**
   - o **Join Relevant Groups**:
   - o Mandy: This is a well-known platform for film and TV professionals. It offers a comprehensive database of industry contacts, including producers.
   - o **Website**: Mandy.com

- **ProductionHub**: A global network for film, video, TV, live event, and post-production professionals, offering a directory of industry contacts.
- **Website**: ProductionHub.com
- **Film & TV Pro**: A platform for connecting with film and TV industry professionals, including producers.
- **Website**: filmandtvpro.com/
- **Women in Film & Television (WFTV)**: This organization supports women in the industry and provides networking opportunities.
- **Website**: wftv.org.uk/
- **Stage 32**: A social network for creative professionals in the film, television, and theatre industries.
- **Website**: stage32.com
- **Film Independent**: This organization offers resources and networking opportunities for independent filmmakers.
- **Website**: filmindependent.org

- **Access the Database**: Use the database to find producers, their interests, and contact information.
- **Reach Out**: Send a personalized message to introduce yourself and propose collaboration.

3. **'Producers to Watch' Lists & Articles**
    - **Find Annual Lists**: Look for lists of up-and-coming producers from sources like the BFI or ScreenDaily.
    - **Research Producers**: Identify producers who make films like yours.
    - **Reach Out**: Contact them through social media or email, mentioning the list and your interest in their work.

Direct Outreach

Proactively reach out to producers you want to work with.

1. **Direct Emails & Messages**
    - **Identify Potential Contacts**: Find producers you want to connect with.

- **Craft a Personalized Message**: Adapt your introduction post to address the individual you're contacting.
    - **Example Message**: "Hi [Name], I admire your work on [Film]. I'm an emerging filmmaker working on a new short film and would love to discuss potential collaboration opportunities with you."

Industry Events and Networking

Attend industry events and networking groups to meet producers in person.

1. **Film Festivals**
    - **Attend Screenings**: Go to screenings of films you're interested in.
    - **Network**: Ask around to see if the producer is attending and introduce yourself.
    - **Follow Up**: If you don't meet the producer in person, reach out online after the festival, mentioning that you watched their film.
2. **Networking Groups**

- **Join Paid Networking Groups**: Consider joining groups like Women in Film and TV.
- **Participate in Events**: Attend networking events to meet serious, professional filmmakers.
- **Engage Actively**: Be proactive in introducing yourself and discussing your projects.

3. **Local Film Offices**
    - **Contact Local Film Offices**: Reach out to your local film office for connections.
    - **Ask for Introductions**: Inquire if they can connect you with local producers.
        - **Example Email**: "Dear [Film Office], I'm a filmmaker in the area and am looking to collaborate with local producers. Could you assist me with any connections?"

4. **Industry Events (In-Person and Online)**
    - **Select the Right Events**: Choose events that are likely to attract producers.
        - **Examples**: Industry panels, producer-specific workshops.

- **Network Effectively**: Introduce yourself and exchange contact information.
- **Follow Up**: Send a thank-you email or message after the event to keep the conversation going.

By following these practical steps and grouping similar methods together, you can effectively connect with producers and build relationships that will help bring your film projects to life. Focus on the methods that best suit your style and preferences, and master them to increase your chances of finding the right producer for your film.

Appendices

Glossary of Filmmaking Terms

Aspect Ratio: The width-to-height ratio of the film's frame.

Blocking: Planning actors' movements in a scene.

Continuity: Consistency in the details from shot to shot.

Dolly Shot: A shot where the camera moves smoothly on a track.

Foley: The reproduction of everyday sound effects added in post-production.

Shot List: A list detailing each shot needed for a scene.

Storyboarding: Creating drawings for each shot to plan a scene visually.

Logline: A brief summary of a film's plot.

Screenplay: The script of a film, including dialogue and descriptions of scenes.

Producer: The person responsible for overseeing the production of a film.

Director of Photography (DP): The person responsible for the visual aspects of a film.

Gaffer: The head of the electrical department, responsible for lighting.

Key Grip: The person in charge of the setup, adjustment, and maintenance of production equipment.

Best Boy: The chief assistant to the gaffer or key grip.

ADR (Automated Dialogue Replacement): The process of re-recording dialogue in post-production.

Colour Grading: The process of enhancing the colour of a film.

Sound Mixing: Combining and adjusting the levels of audio tracks.

Montage: A sequence of shots edited together to condense time or convey information quickly.

Master Shot: A continuous shot that captures the entire action of a scene.

Close-Up (CU): A shot that tightly frames a person or object.

Medium Shot (MS): A shot that frames a subject from the waist up.

Wide Shot (WS): A shot that shows the subject within their surrounding environment.

Over-the-Shoulder Shot (OTS): A shot looking over a character's shoulder at another subject.

Two-Shot: A shot with two subjects in the frame.

Match Cut: A cut that preserves continuity between two shots.

Jump Cut: A cut that interrupts continuity to create a jarring effect.

Pan: A horizontal camera movement.

Tilt: A vertical camera movement.

Zoom: Changing the focal length of the lens to give the illusion of moving closer to or further from the subject.

Rack Focus: Changing the focus of the lens during a shot to shift attention between subjects.

Resource List
Books:
"In the Blink of an Eye" by Walter Murch

"Directing Actors" by Judith Weston

"Save the Cat!" by Blake Snyder

"On Directing Film" by David Mamet

"The Lean Forward Moment" by Norman Hollyn

"Film Directing Shot by Shot" by Steven Katz

The Director's Cut: A Journal for Filmmakers

Websites:
https://www.studiobinder.com/

https://nofilmschool.com/

https://filmfreeway.com/

https://www.withoutabox.com/

https://www.colorgradingcentral.com/

https://www.sounddogs.com/

https://freesound.org/

https://www.videocopilot.net/

https://fxhome.com/

https://handbrake.fr/

https://www.apple.com/final-cut-pro/compressor/

https://partnerhelp.netflixstudios.com/hc/en-us/sections/1500000676722-Cameras-Image-Capture
https://www.bbc.co.uk/commissioning/tv/production/technical-specification.shtml
https://www.mandy.com/
https://www.productionhub.com/
https://www.themill.com/
https://www.company3.com/
https://www.bydeluxe.com/
https://videodirect.amazon.com/home/landing
https://shorts.tv/
https://www.indierights.com/
https://www.reddit.com/r/Filmmakers/
https://www.stage32.com/

Further Reading and Learning Paths

Screenwriting: "Save the Cat!" by Blake Snyder
Directing: "On Directing Film" by David Mamet
Editing: "The Lean Forward Moment" by Norman Hollyn

Acknowledgments
Thank you to everyone who has supported me on this journey. From mentors and colleagues to friends and family, your encouragement and guidance have been invaluable.

About the Author
Steve McCarten is an accomplished filmmaker and educator. With experience in directing, writing, and teaching at Bournemouth University, Steve has dedicated his career to storytelling and nurturing new talent in the film industry. You can reach Steve via his website www.stevemccarten.com or follow him on Twitter @SteveMcCarten.

Copyright © 2024 by Steve McCarten

All rights reserved. This book is protected under the copyright laws of the United States and other countries. Unauthorized duplication, distribution, or transmission of this book in any form or by any means, including photocopying, recording, or other electronic or mechanical methods, without prior written permission from the author is prohibited.

For permission to use excerpts or material from this book, contact:
www.stevemccarten.com

Disclaimer: The information in this book is based on the author's personal experience and research. While every effort has been made to ensure accuracy, the author and publisher assume no responsibility for errors or omissions, or for any damages resulting from the use of the information contained herein.

Printed in Great Britain
by Amazon

48215786R00079